Vol. 20
No. 213

Suppandi - Testing Times..2
Deng Finds A Bride..3-5
Kalia The Crow - Doob Doob Climbs A Tree!.................6-10
Tinkle Times..13
Raju's Cycle..14-15
Janoo And Wooly Woo In Weather Witch....................16-21
The Fox And The Crane...22-23
It Happened To Me...24-25
Ha...Ha...Hee...Hee...Ho...Ho!!...............................26-27
The Challenge...29-33
Shikari Shambu's Swashbuckling Adventure................34-38
Young Poets' Corner..39
Prachi's Fun Recipes: Idli Faces.......................................40
Prachi's Vegetable Craft: Elephant..................................41
Tinkle Digest Mailbox..42
The Hilsa Adventure...43-48
Suppandi: Short Cut..49
The Lion Cub..50-53
Tinkle Tells You Why..54-55
Fun Time..56-57
The Magic Cart Adventure..59-64
Adventures Of Doob Doob -
The Commanding Personality...65-69
The First Flying Vertebrates: Pterosaurs.......................70-71
Tinkle Picture Quiz...72-73
Ina, Mina, Mynah, Mo - Green Fingers..........................75-80
Chinnu Sets A Trap...81-87

9

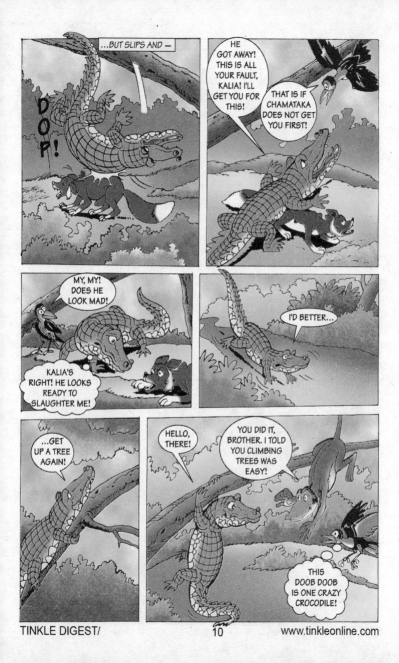

EVERY TINKLE EVER
ONE CLASSIC SERIES

TINKLE TIMES

Coconut pierced with a finger (Malaysia)

Ho Eng Hui, a Kung Fu master, created a Malaysian record by breaking four different coconuts by piercing them with his index finger. He performed the feat in front of a crowd in Malacca, in a little more than 30 seconds. In the process he bettered his own previous record of breaking three coconuts in 70 seconds. He is now preparing to enter the Guinness Book of World Records.

Meteor strikes boy (Germany)

Fourteen-year-old Gerrit Blank was hit by a meteor on his way to school but escaped with a scar on his hand. Gerrit saw a fireball dropping from the sky. The pea-sized meteor struck his hand and then hit the ground with a loud bang, leaving a foot-wide crater. Chances of being struck by a meteor are one in a million since most of them burn away in the atmosphere and the rest fall in water.

Caravan thieves surprised (Sweden)

Thieves in Skovde tried to make off with a caravan by hitching it to their car. However, they did not realise that the owner of the vehicle was asleep inside. Bjorn Feldbaek, awoke to find his vehicle on the move. When the thieves stopped to enter the caravan, he screamed so loudly that the thieves were startled out of their wits. They fled on foot leaving their car behind.

RAJU'S CYCLE

Based on a story sent by:
Sabir Salam,
Thiruvananthapuram, Kerala.

Illustrations:
Kishore Govilkar

www.tinkleonline.com

18

19 TINKLE DIGEST/

www.tinkleonline.com

21

THE FOX AND THE CRANE

Readers' Choice
Based on a story sent by:
Apratim Gole
Kothrud, Pune - 411 029.

Illustrations:
Archana Amberkar

TINKLE TO THE RESCUE

I used to get a daily allowance of Rs 6/-, which I kept in a small pocket in my schoolbag. I would buy a samosa in the recess from the school canteen everyday. I used to save the rest of the money.

One day when I came back to the classroom after recess I found the remaining money missing from my bag. This went on for a number of days. My mother advised me to keep the money in my trouser pocket. As expected the robberies stopped and my money was safe but I still wanted to find out who the thief was.

Some days later, I found a very old issue of Tinkle at my friend's house. I started reading it and found the Mopes and Purr story very interesting. In it, the detective duo caught a thief by luring him. It struck me that I could catch the thief in my class by using a similar method.

So, on a day when all my classmates were present, I announced to everyone that I had 50 rupees in my school bag. During recess, I left the classroom but kept watch from a window. Soon a boy approached my bag and opened the small pocket but naturally found nothing. Imagine his horror when he found me standing behind him, smiling. He started shivering and stammering and confessed to taking the money. I asked him to return all my money, which he later did. It was in Tinkle No. 328 that I'd read the Mopes and Purr story and that got me hooked on to Tinkle.

Based on a true-life incident sent by :
Sameer N. Patkar, Mumbai - 400 071.

IT HAPPENED TO ME

BOURNVITA BABY

When I was very small, I was extremely fond of eating chocolate powder. My mother used to keep the bottle containing Bournvita away from me. One day, luck smiled upon me. I found the bottle of Bournvita unattended on the dining table. I climbed on a dining chair and inverted the bottle into my mouth. I swallowed a large quantity of the powder and choked! The powder went into my windpipe and I was breathless; unable to speak also. I ran to my mother who was in the backyard. She hit me hard on my back and a large lump of the Bournvita powder was flung out of my mouth. My mother saved me from a horrible accident.

Based on a true-life incident sent by: **Mohd Umar Rehman,** Aligarh, U.P.

BOARD CONFUSION

This incident occurred when I went shopping with my dad when I was in the third standard. My father met one of his friends in the market place and started chatting with him. They were chatting in front of two shops that had just a wall between them. One of them was a shop selling chocolates and the other, sarees. I went into the shop selling chocolates and asked for a chocolate. The shopkeeper told me how much it cost. I then asked for a 40% discount as the board outside the shop said "40% Discount". At this everybody in the shop burst out laughing. My father came in just then and I related the happenings to him. He too burst out laughing. Finally, the shopkeeper controlled his laughter and informed me that the board outside was for the shop selling sarees. When I went out and checked the board, it said, "40% Discount on Sarees!"

Based on a true-life incident sent by : **P. Sankar Doth,** Andhra Pradesh.

LAUGH WITH LITTLE SUPPANDI !

Something Fishy

SEEK NEW ADVENTURES THIS SUMMER!

Prepare yourself for fun and adventure!

Discover worlds of exciting escapades

Engage in mind-boggling puzzles

Keep yourself entertained with amusing games and DIYs

Brace yourself for an ultra fun ride!

*THE HOLE ON TOP OF THE WHALE'S HEAD THROUGH WHICH IT BREATHES

YOUNG POETS' CORNER

I Wish I Were Up There

I wish I were up there
Up there in the skies
The solar system my school
The earth my classroom
And the sun my playground

I wish I were up there
So that I could hop across stars
And the shooting ones
Would be my cars
No money just love
As free as a dove

I wish I were up there
So that I could sleep on the moon
There would be no morning and no afternoon
My teardrops would be rain
And my smiles would destroy pain

Aakriti Pasricha
VII 'B', Bluebells International School

The Earth

Don't destroy the earth
It's already so bare
Don't cut down trees
To them, it isn't fair.

If you were in their place,
Wouldn't you like to live?
Trees are so helpful to us
But what do humans give?

Humans are ungrateful
And simply couldn't care less
Even if the earth turned barren
And it became a mess.

Don't destroy the earth
It all reflects on us
Saving the earth and all the trees
Is a great big must.

Stuti Johri
10 years
Mumbai

Happiness

Happiness in the green meadow
Where the flowers bloom
Happiness in my humble home
Also in my room

Happiness for the birds that fly
For the dogs that bark
Happiness in the lovely swings
When I am in the park

Eesha Roy Chowdhury
8 years

PRACHI'S FUN RECIPES

IDLI FACES

You will need:
Idlis
Mint Leaves (Quarter cup)
Coriander Leaves (Half cup)
Cumin Seeds (1 Teaspoon)
Ginger – finely chopped (Half teaspoon)
Garlic (Single clove)
Green Chillies (Two)
Salt
Grated Carrot
Tomato Sauce

Instructions:

1. First, you need to make the green chutney. For this, put mint leaves, coriander leaves, green chillies, ginger, garlic, cumin seeds and salt together in the mixer and grind.
2. Slice the idli horizontally into half, as shown. Spread the green chutney over one half.
3. Place the other half over it. For the face, draw eyes with the green chutney over the idli.
4. For the mouth, use tomato sauce.
5. Spread some pasteurized butter on the idli, above the eyes. Place either grated carrot or coriander leaves for the hair, over the butter.
6. The idli faces are ready.

PRACHI'S VEGETABLE CRAFT
ELEPHANT

You will need:

Brinjal, Beetroots, Carrots, Ivy Gourds *(Tendli)*, Cloves, Toothpicks

Instructions:

1. Take a big brinjal and cut off a slice from its rounded front portion. Insert two toothpicks, as shown.

2. Next, take a beetroot and slice off a piece from it too. Insert two toothpicks.

3. Now, fix the beetroot to the brinjal with the help of the inserted toothpicks.

4. Pluck out the leafy part around the brinjal's stalk.

5. Take two circular slices from another beetroot and fix these with toothpicks to the head of the elephant, for ears.

5. Cut two pieces from a carrot (one medium-sized and one small), as shown. Attach these to the bottom of the elephant's head. This is the trunk.

6. Next, cut equal-sized stubs from carrots and fix these to the bottom of the brinjal. These are the elephant's legs.

7. For the eyes, cut two circular pieces from an ivy gourd *(tendli)*. Attach these on the head of the elephant on either side, using two cloves.

8. Your vegetable elephant is ready for display!

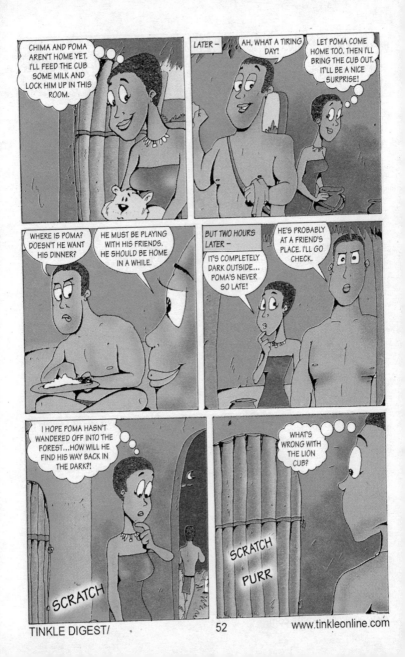

52

Is it true that a person sitting in a boat in the ocean would not notice if a tsunami passed under him?
—Samuel N.,
Mumbai – 400 080.

Tsunamis are caused by under-sea movements called seaquakes. When a seaquake occurs at a particular location, the water nearby is agitated and sends waves in all directions. The speed depends on the depth of water. The deeper the water, the lesser the resistance and so the speed is high and the size of the waves is small. Hence, most tsunamis go undetected in the open sea. However, the same wave approaching shallow water near the shore slows down and increases in size and may form a wall of water more than 30 metres high.

What is meant by an Electroencephalogram?
— R. Uday Bhaskar,
Andhra Pradesh.

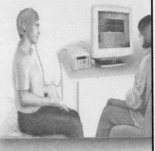

An electroencephalogram is the recording of electrical activity by neurons (nerve cells) in the brain. To produce an electroencephalogram, electrodes are attached to the patient's scalp and the recording is done on a long moving chart using ink pens that oscillate with the changes in the brain's electrical activity. This instrument is called an electroencephalograph. It is commonly used to diagnose and study epilepsy.

Why should calcium be a necessary part of our diet?

—R. Srinivas, *Bengaluru.*

Calcium is extremely important in the formation and health of bones and teeth.
Calcium is also important for good muscle tone. Since the heart is the most powerful muscle, calcium is necessary for the proper functioning of the heart.

For the proper absorption of calcium by the body, the diet should also contain vitamins C and D, and phosphorus.

Food sources high in calcium include milk, cheese, green leafy vegetables and clams and oysters.

While Earth rotates, does the atmosphere rotate with it? If yes, why?

—Manish K. Majumdhar, *Orissa.*

The atmosphere does rotate along with the Earth. It is the gravitational pull exercised by Earth that keeps the atmosphere bound to the planet.

FUN TIME

(I) Hidden in this word, scrambled diagonally, horizontally and vertically are the names of 10 famous characters from different books, stories and fairy tales. Use the clues below to find them.

K	P	E	T	E	R	P	A	N
U	I	D	W	A	E	A	L	I
M	N	B	R	F	G	R	I	P
S	O	B	M	A	B	X	C	N
W	C	W	R	Z	C	C	E	I
A	C	V	G	A	K	U	F	L
M	H	V	R	L	J	T	L	A
I	I	U	I	L	I	B	I	A
T	O	M	S	A	W	Y	E	R
B	U	P	L	D	V	E	R	G
G	U	L	L	I	V	E	R	N
R	A	P	U	N	Z	E	L	I

Clues:

1. The boy who lived in Never-Never Land.
2. His nose grew longer whenever he lied.
3. This 'man-cub' was raised in the jungle by a family of wolves.
4. When he rubbed the magic lamp, a genie appeared.
5. She was asked to let her long, golden hair down from a tower.
6. He is the most famous vampire in history.
7. He visited Lilliput and Brobdingnag on his travels.
8. An adventurous boy who lived in Malgudi with his friends.
9. He and his best friend Huckleberry Finn have had many adventures.
10. She fell through a rabbit hole into Wonderland.

II) Anagrams are words that can be rearranged to form other new words. For example, 'pea' can be rearranged to make 'ape'. Janoo and Wooly Woo are trying to change the following words into new magical words. Help them solve these anagrams, using the clues given below.

E.g: PAN = go to sleep = NAP

1. DAWN = a witch's magical tool =

2. ACT = a witch's favourite pet =

3. OPTION = a witch's magic brew =

4. MARCH = a witch's magic formula or spell =

5. CURES = a witch's hex =

Activity
MAKE YOUR OWN JIGSAW PUZZLE

Do you like jigsaw puzzles? Are the ones you buy too easy or too difficult for you? Here's how to make your own fun jigsaw puzzle - exactly the way you want it!

What you need: A colourful magazine or calendar picture, a thin sheet of cardboard, pencil, a pair of scissors and glue.

How to go about it:

1. Place your picture on the cardboard. Trace the outline of your picture onto the cardboard.
2. Cut the cardboard to the same size as your picture.
3. Glue your picture onto the cardboard, making sure you press the picture onto the cardboard firmly.
4. Once the glue has dried, cut the cardboard with the picture on it into irregularly shaped pieces. Ask an adlut to help you with this.
5. If you want your puzzle to be easy, you can keep the pieces large. But if you want a tougher challenge, cut the cardboard into smaller pieces.
6. After you have cut up the entire picture, mix together the pieces.
7. Your jigsaw puzzle is now ready!

Tip: You can make a jigsaw puzzle using a poster of your favourite sports star or film celebrity!

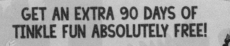

www.tinkleonline.com

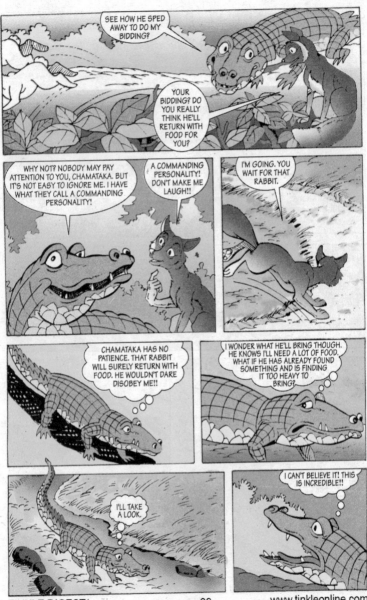

The First Flying Vertebrates: PTEROSAURS

Script: Luis Fernandes

Illustrations, Colouring and Layout : Jitendra Patil

EARTH FILE

Living as the same time as the dinosaurs (and related to them) were reptiles that could fly!

Scientists have named them Pterosaurs - Greek words meaning 'winged lizards'. There was great diversity among them: some were as small as modern day pigeons; others were the size of small airplanes. With a wingspan of over 18 metres!

Pterosaurs generally had long, flat heads, and in the bigger species the heads were enormous – the size of the front door of a house.

The pterosaurs could fly very well and were the masters of the skies. They were the first vertebrates to fly, and for several million years (until the first birds appeared) the only ones to do so. They were also the largest creatures that ever flew.

Their wings were not made up of feathers but were thin, leathery membranes stretching from the side of the body to the side of the fourth finger on the forelimb.

This finger was extremely long. The three other digits on the forelimb were of normal size.

While some of them lived on insects, others preyed on fish and other animals found in the oceans. Some may have scavenged on dead animals on land.

The pterosaurs faded out at the same time as the dinosaurs, 65 million years ago. By that time another set of vertebrates had established themselves in the skies: the birds.

Today, there are no flying reptiles in existence. However, there are reptiles that can glide from tree to tree and from tree to ground. They glide such great distances that they seem to fly. So though they are just gliders they're called 'Flying Reptiles'. These include the flying lizard, and the flying snake.

TINKLE PICTURE QUIZ

(I) Match the rivers (1 – 4) with their location (a – d).

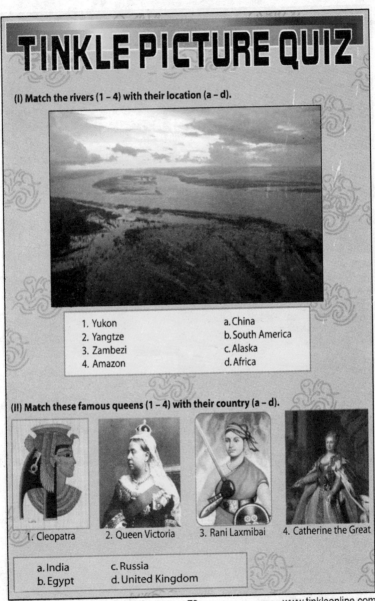

1. Yukon
2. Yangtze
3. Zambezi
4. Amazon

a. China
b. South America
c. Alaska
d. Africa

(II) Match these famous queens (1 – 4) with their country (a – d).

1. Cleopatra
2. Queen Victoria
3. Rani Laxmibai
4. Catherine the Great

a. India
b. Egypt
c. Russia
d. United Kingdom

www.tinkleonline.com

(III) Match the wheels (1 – 4) with the modes of transport (a – d) they are part of.

a. Tractor   b. Motorcycle   c. Bicycle   d. Bullock Cart

(IV) Match the famous personalities each of whose first name is Charles (1 – 4) with what they are famous for (a – d).

1. Charles Darwin   2. Charles Dickens   3. Charles Babbage   4. Charles Chaplin

a. Uniquely humorous films
b. Theory of Evolution
c. Written works
d. Invention of computers

Answers to Picture Quiz
(I)	1-c, 2-a, 3-d, 4-b
(II)	1-b, 2-d, 3-a, 4-c
(III)	1-c, 2-d, 3-a, 4-b
(IV)	1-b, 2-c, 3-d, 4-a

www.tinkleonline.com

www.tinkleonline.com

MONKEY KERCHIEF STAND

You will need:

- Tinted Sheets (Black, Red and Pink colours)
- Black Sketch Pen
- Glue
- A Set of Handkerchiefs

Instructions:

1. Take the black tinted sheet and cut out a rectangle 'A' (length = 12 cm; breadth = 10 cm) and two identical squares 'E' (side = 8 cm), as shown. Cut the edges of the squares 'E' and roll each of them into cylindrical wheels, as shown.

2. From the red tinted sheet, cut out a rectangle 'B' (length = 12 cm; breadth = 10 cm) and two identical squares 'D' (side = 6 cm) and two smaller rectangles 'G' (length = 8 cm; breadth = 5 cm), as shown.

3. Next, from the pink tinted sheet, cut out a rectangle 'C' (length = 10 cm; breadth = 8 cm) and a bigger rectangle 'F' (length = 24 cm; breadth = 12 cm), as shown.

4. Fold the pink rectangle 'F' into half.

5. On these rectangles and squares 'A' to 'G', draw and cut the respective shapes, as shown.

6. Afterwards, stick the red oval over the pink heart shape; next, stick this over the black oval. Attach the two small red circles behind the black oval, for ears.

7. Draw eyes, nose and mouth with a black sketch pen – the monkey's face is ready.

8. Glue the monkey's face to the pink quadrilateral, as shown. Next, stick both the black cylindrical wheels to the front of the pink quadrilateral.

9. Finally, attach the two paws to the other end of each black cylindrical wheel. Place a few kerchiefs over the cylindrical wheel, as shown.

10. The monkey-shaped kerchief stand is ready!

TINKLE
Digest

Vol. 21
No. 214

Nasruddin Hodja - The Portrait...2-4

The Original Prankster...5-12

World's Most Popular Sport...15-16

Kalia The Crow - Chamataka! Chamataka!.................................17-21

Philemon and Baucis...22-26

Beware of the Snake...27

It Happened To Me...**28-29**

Tinkle Picture Quiz...**30-31**

Tantri The Mantri - Tantri and the Bees.................................32-35

A Queen Fights Back...36-38

Snip, Snip...39-40

The Peacock...41-44

Tinkle Tells You Why...**46-47**

Prachi's Fun Recipes...**48**

Prachi's Vegetable Kraft...**49**

Shikari Shambu - Revenge of the Mummy.................................50-54

Suppandi - The Oil Stain...55

The Greedy Masseur...56-59

Ha...Ha...Hee...Hee...Ho...Ho!!...**60-61**

Tinkle Times...**62**

Young Poets' Corner...**63**

The King's Successor...65-75

The Elephant and the Mouse...76-77

The Human Species...78-79

Tinkle Digest Mailbox...**80**

Tinkle Fun Time...**82-83**

Sindbad, the Sailor...84-87

6

8

Pet Problem
A Little Suppandi Tale

Readers' Choice

Based on an idea sent by:
S. Akaash, Thrissur, Kerala.

Illustrations: Prachi Killekar

WORLD'S MOST POPULAR SPORT!

Football is the world's most popular sport, followed by millions of people in more than 160 countries!

GAME BASICS

Two teams of 11 players each, take part in a football match. The match is divided into two periods of 45 minutes each. The team that scores the maximum goals in these two periods wins the game. A player can use his feet or even head, basically any part of his body except the hands and arms. That is strictly prohibited!

HOW IT ALL BEGAN

A Chinese military manual dating back to the 2nd or 3rd century BC shows what was perhaps the earliest form of football. It was called *Tsui Chu*. The player had to kick a leather ball filled with feathers and hair into a small net. The Romans are also said to have encouraged a similar game as part of military training.

There is a historical account of a football match played near London in 1175. In the beginning, football matches were unruly games played on the streets with no proper teams. In fact, Edward II, King of England banned football in 1314 since it had no regard for people or property. Football was banned many times but somehow people never lost interest in it. It was only by the 1800s that the game began to be played in upper class schools where its first rules were drawn.

Football was introduced in India during the days of the British Empire. The Mohun Bagan Athletic Club established on August 15, 1889 in Bengal is still going strong. It is considered one of the oldest football clubs in Asia today.

The first few football matches were played between the different army teams. In 1911 the Mohun Bagan team became the first Indian football team to defeat a British team, the Eastern Yorkshire Regiment. The club gained a lot of popularity after this victory.

The Indian football team has won gold medals at the 1951 and 1962 Asian Games. Football is extremely popular in Goa, Kerala and Kolkata.

India's best known footballer is Baichung Bhutia.

THE FOOTBALL ASSOCIATION AND THE WORLD CUP

FIFA - The Fédération Internationale de Football Association, is the world-governing body for football. FIFA organises the World Cup every four years. Its headquarters are in Zurich, Switzerland.

FIFA was founded by seven European nations in 1904. But it was later in the 1920s that a group of French football administrators thought of bringing together the world's strongest national football teams to compete for the title of World Champions.

The FIFA World Cup is held every four years in the chosen host country. The elimination process for the World Cup begins two years in advance. Initially, World Cups used to be held only in European countries or the Americas. But lately, they have been held in Asian countries as well. The FIFA World Cup (2002) was held in Korea and Japan. Germany hosted for World Cup 2006.

The mascot for the World Cup 2006 was Goleo VI, the thinking, talking lion, and his companion, Pille, the talking football.

FIFA FACT FILE

- The first FIFA World Cup was held in Uruguay, in 1930.

- Uruguay were the first country to win the FIFA World Cup when they defeated Argentina in the finals in 1930.

- Just Fontaine (France), holds a record of 13 goals at the 1958 FIFA World Cup held in Sweden. This record hasn't been broken yet!

- Only seven countries have ever won the World Cup: Uruguay, Argentina, Brazil, Gemany, Italy, France and England.

- Brazil won the FIFA World Cup in 2002, and is the country with most victories - they have won the World Cup five times! Italy is second, with four World Cup titles. Germany has won three times.

- The present FIFA World Cup Trophy was inaugurated in 1974. The World Cup before that was awarded permanently to Brazil when they won it for the third time in 1970.

Brazil has won the World Cup five times!

NO, NO! I ALREADY HAVE THE ANSWER! WE CAN PREVENT THEM FROM RUNNING AWAY BY DISGUISING OURSELVES AS HARMLESS BEINGS! YOU GOT IT? IF THEY THINK WE'RE HARMLESS THEY WON'T RUN AWAY, AND THEN WE CAN CATCH THEM EASILY! WHAT DO YOU THINK OF MY IDEA?

DO ME A FAVOUR, DOOB DOOB! NEXT TIME YOU GET AN IDEA...

... KEEP IT SECRET! I ONLY HOPE I CAN FIND THOSE RABBITS AGAIN!!

WHAT'S WRONG, DOOB DOOB? CHAMATAKA SEEMS UPSET.

I TOLD HIM WE SHOULD DISGUISE OURSELVES SO THAT ANIMALS WON'T SUSPECT WE'RE OUT TO CATCH THEM, BUT HE WOULDN'T LISTEN!

KALIA!

ER... KALIA, DO YOU KNOW HOW I COULD DISGUISE MYSELF?

WHAT DO YOU WANT TO DISGUISE YOURSELF AS?

WELL, I THOUGHT IF I COULD DISGUISE MYSELF AS A BUSH I COULD CREEP UP TO AN UNSUSPECTING RABBIT... I...I MEAN TO SOME ANIMAL WHO IS NOT YOUR FRIEND.... I WOULDN'T DREAM OF HURTING ANY OF YOUR FRIENDS, YOU UNDERSTAND?

YES, YES... LET ME THINK...

DISGUISING YOURSELF AS A BUSH MIGHT NOT BE EASY. BUT YOU COULD EASILY DISGUISE YOURSELF AS A HEAP OF LEAVES.

A HEAP OF LEAVES? HOW?

18

21

PHILEMON AND BAUCIS

A Greek tale

Script: Lopamudra   Illustrations: C.M. Vitankar

TAK TAK

TWO STRANGERS ONCE CAME TO A VILLAGE CALLED PYRGIA.

MAY WE COME IN?

BANG

THEY WENT TO ALL THE HOUSES IN THE VILLAGE BUT THE SAME THING HAPPENED EVERYWHERE.

WELL?

THERE IS ONE SMALL HUT OUT THERE. LET'S TRY THAT ONE TOO.

THEY WALKED UP TO THE HUT.

WHY! THIS LITTLE DOOR IS WIDE OPEN!

WHO'S THERE?

WE ARE TRAVELLERS IN SEARCH OF...

COME IN! COME IN!

WELCOME, FRIENDS. YOU LOOK TIRED AND HUNGRY.

22

24

IT HAPPENED TO ME

HONESTY PAYS

Once when I was in the sixth standard, I found someone's calculator lying in the school grounds. I picked it up and gave it to our headmaster. He made an announcement on the school stage, asking the owner to come and collect the calculator. He also called me on the stage and praised me for my honesty. All the other students congratulated me that day.

Based on a true-life incident sent by M. Sufujan Ahmed Faizi, Chennai - 600 014

Based on a true-life incident sent by Arushi Verma, Mumbai - 400 053.

BRAVE RESCUE

Once I had gone for a picnic with my cousin and his family. While the others were getting ready, my cousin and I went ahead and sat in the car with the doors open. The area wasn't well developed, and stray cattle roamed the landscape. Suddenly, we saw a bull rushing towards our car! I closed the door quickly, but to my horror, the other door was still wide open. My cousin was terrified and started crying. No sooner had I leaned over and closed the door on his side than the bull struck, breaking the car window. It quietly walked away after that. We were scared, but safe. I quietened my cousin and then told the adults about the horror we had experienced.

IT HAPPENED TO ME

MOONLIGHT ADVENTURE

I was in the fifth standard when this incident took place. One bright, moonlit night my two older brothers challenged me to a race on the road. I was confident and accepted their challenge. We started the race. I had hardly gone a few metres when I tripped on something and fell with a thud. My brothers had tied a rope to trip me, and were now laughing their heads off. I started crying. My father heard me and came out. He scolded my brothers a lot when he saw what they had done. That day I also learnt not to show off.

Based on a true-life incident sent by Thekrusolie Vakha, Kohima, Nagaland.

MUDDLED MEMORY

Once when my mother was out she telephoned me and told me to take some money from her drawer and buy a tube of toothpaste. I spoke to a friend on the phone and then went to the shop. The shopkeeper made me wait for a few minutes because he didn't have toothpaste. When he finally got me a tube, I asked for the balance money. He said I hadn't given him any money at all. I was sure I had and an argument ensued. Finally I left in a huff. When I reached home, I saw my mother standing by the door with the money. I had forgotten to take it with me! I rushed back, paid the shopkeeper and apologised

to him. It was the most embarrassing moment of my life.

Based on a true-life incident sent by Rohit Nayak, Kolkata, West Bengal.

TINKLE PICTURE QUIZ

I. Match the animals (1 – 4) with the descriptions (a – d).

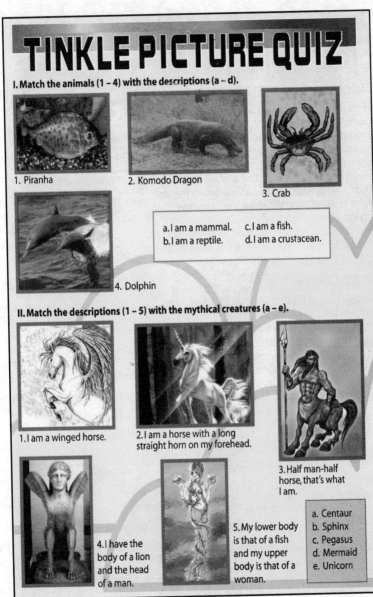

1. Piranha

2. Komodo Dragon

3. Crab

a. I am a mammal.   c. I am a fish.
b. I am a reptile.   d. I am a crustacean.

4. Dolphin

II. Match the descriptions (1 – 5) with the mythical creatures (a – e).

1. I am a winged horse.

2. I am a horse with a long straight horn on my forehead.

3. Half man-half horse, that's what I am.

4. I have the body of a lion and the head of a man.

5. My lower body is that of a fish and my upper body is that of a woman.

a. Centaur
b. Sphinx
c. Pegasus
d. Mermaid
e. Unicorn

30

III. Match the pioneers (1 – 4) with their areas of expertise (a – d).

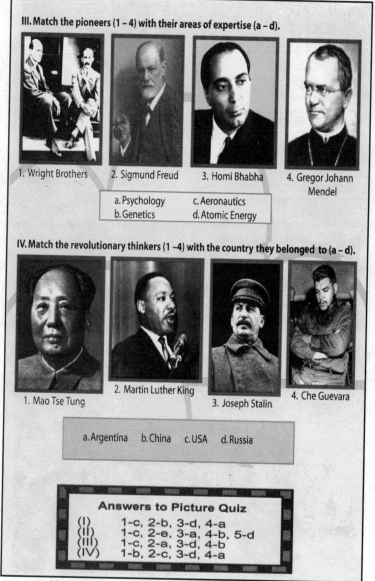

1. Wright Brothers
2. Sigmund Freud
3. Homi Bhabha
4. Gregor Johann Mendel

a. Psychology   c. Aeronautics
b. Genetics   d. Atomic Energy

IV. Match the revolutionary thinkers (1 –4) with the country they belonged to (a – d).

1. Mao Tse Tung
2. Martin Luther King
3. Joseph Stalin
4. Che Guevara

a. Argentina   b. China   c. USA   d. Russia

Answers to Picture Quiz

(I)   1-c, 2-b, 3-d, 4-a
(II) 1-c, 2-e, 3-a, 4-b, 5-d
(III) 1-c, 2-a, 3-d, 4-b
(IV) 1-b, 2-c, 3-d, 4-a

34 www.tinkleonline.com

SNIP, SNIP

Based on a story sent by: **Th. Tamphasana,** Leirak, Imphal.

Illustrations: **Abhijeet Kini**

The Peacock

A Tale from Uzbekistan

Script: Luis Fernandes
Illustrations: Gajoo Tayde

THE KHAN OF MORGOLO WAS FOND OF CLOTHES.

HE HAD A HUNDRED WEAVERS AND A HUNDRED TAILORS AND THEY HAD TO MAKE A NEW ROBE FOR HIM EVERYDAY.

IT'S A TRIFLE UNCOMFORTABLE UNDER MY LEFT ARM...

...HANG THE TAILORS WHO MADE IT!

YES, MY LORD!

EVERY EVENING, HE WOULD WALK UP AND DOWN THE STREET LEADING TO HIS PALACE.

PEOPLE WERE FORCED TO STAND AND WATCH AND APPLAUD.

SPLENDID!

OOOOH!

I'VE NEVER SEEN ANYTHING LIKE IT BEFORE.

ADMIRATION WAS COMPULSORY!

THEN, ONE DAY, A SHOCKING THING HAPPENED!

OH, WHAT A BORE!

42

How is stained glass made?

- Sapna Bhat, *D/O S.G. Bhat, No. 249, 8th Main, 9th Block, Nagarbhavi II Stage, Bengaluru – 560 072.*

Coloured glass or stained glass is made by adding certain oxides to the glass. Nickel oxide produces tints ranging from yellow to purple (depending on the base glass), while cobalt oxide gives an intense blue. Many other attractive colours can be produced with other chemicals.

What are Maglev trains? How do they work?

- Lathika A.K. *Panangottu Veedu, Choozampala, Mukkola P.O., Thiruvananthapuram – 695 044, Kerala.*

Maglev is the shortened form of 'Magnetic Levitation'. In a Maglev train, levitation (lifting into the air) is achieved by magnetic repulsion between the magnets on the undercarriage of the train, and induced currents in aluminium coils or sheets that are set in the guideway (rails). Once the train is levitated, power is supplied to other magnetic coils in the guideway walls. This creates a unique system of magnetic fields that pull and push the train along the guideway. Maglev trains float on a cushion of air, eliminating friction. Lack of friction allows these trains to travel at speeds of more than 500 km per hour.

Why do ripe fruits fall off trees?

- Leireesha Correa,
Livlin Cottage, Parapade House, Ashok Nagar Post, Derebail, Mangalore – 575 006.

A plant hormone known as abscisic acid causes the stalk of the fruit to get detached from the stem when the fruit is ripe and ready to be plucked.

Abscisic acid also causes leaves to fall when they have outlived their usefulness. Another hormone called ethylene, which is in gaseous form, helps the fruit to ripen. In the ripening process, the tissues of the fruit become soft and the organic acids are converted into sugars, making the ripe fruit sweet. The fruit also develops aroma or flavour. So it is these two hormones produced by plants that cause fruits to ripen and then to fall.

Why do we sweat?

- William Vanglua, *J.N.V. Tuimom, Churachandpur Dist, Manipur – 795 128.*

We sweat to lose heat. Sweating itself does not reduce body heat but when the sweat evaporates, it takes heat from the body. As the temperature of the body has to be maintained at about 98° F, we may sweat in cool weather too. When it is cool, the small amount of sweat produced evaporates almost as soon as it is formed and we don't realise that we are sweating.

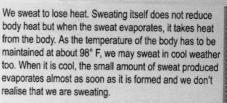

PRACHI'S FUN RECIPES

POHA BHEL

You will need:

Nylon *Poha* or Rice Flakes (200 gms serve 5 persons)
Roasted *Papads* (two)
Oil (Four tablespoons)
Onion (One – Big-sized)
Tomatoes (Two – Medium-sized)
Lemon Juice (One tablespoon)
Coriander
Chaat Masala (Half a teaspoon)
Chilli Powder (Quarter teaspoon)
Salt (To taste)

Instructions:

1. Finely chop the tomatoes, onion and coriander.
2. Put the vegetables in a big bowl. Crush the *papad* and sprinkle.
3. Add oil, *chaat masala*, chilli powder, lemon juice and salt as per taste, to the vegetables. Mix well.

4. Add nylon poha or rice flakes to the mixture. Mix well again.

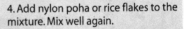

5. The crispy *poha bhel* is ready to be served and eaten.

PRACHI'S
VEGETABLE CRAFT
ORANGE UMBRELLA

You will need:

Orange, Spring Onion, Drinking Straw, Knife, A Pair of Scissors, Cutter, Toothpicks

Instructions:

1. Take the semicircular rind of an orange. Using a knife, carefully make a small hole at the top of the rind, as shown.

2. Insert a drinking straw from above into this hole. Using a cutter, cut the top portion into four parts, to form a four-bladed fan shape, as shown.

3. Next, take a stalk of the spring onion and insert the bottom end of the drinking straw into this stalk. The stalk will form a green covering for the straw. Cut off unnecessary extensions, if any.

4. Take some more stalks of the spring onion. Cut them at a length such that they run from the small hole on top to the rind's circumference.

5. Fix each of these stalks, as shown, using small pieces of toothpicks. These form the spikes of the umbrella.

6. Now attach each of the four blades of the drinking straw to the top of the orange rind with toothpick pieces.

7. Show off your brand new orange umbrella to your family and friends!

www.tinkleonline.com

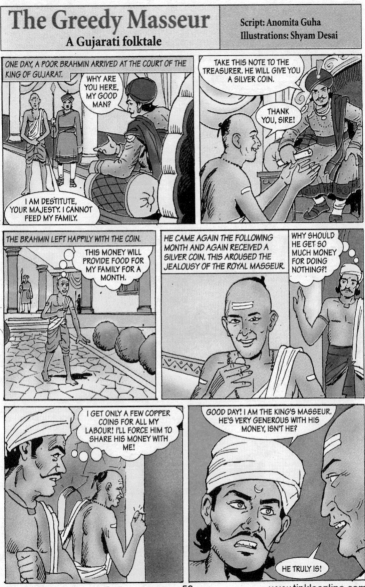

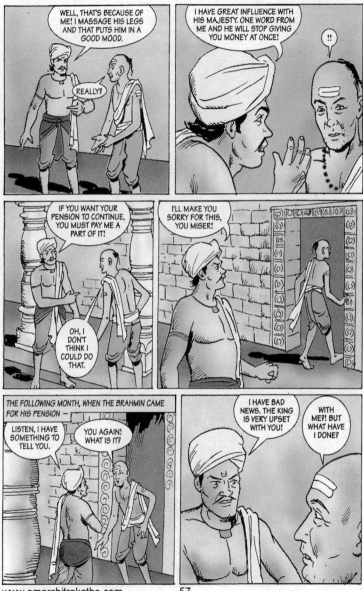

58

TINKLE TIMES

Beluga whale to the rescue (China)

Yang Yun was taking part in a diving competition at the Harbin Polar Land theme park in Heilongjiang, China. Participants were required to dive to a depth of six metres in a pool without the help of breathing equipment. When Yun dived to a depth of four metres, she developed severe leg cramps.

She began to choke and would have drowned had not a beluga whale come to her rescue. Mila, the beluga whale, sensed Yun's distress and pushed her to the surface. Yun eventually made a second attempt after recovering.

Classroom in an aeroplane (The UK)

Children at Kingsland Primary School in Stoke-on-Trent are studying in a unique classroom – a discarded S-360 aeroplane! The children were given a chance to choose the site for an extra classroom. They saw the S-360 plane abandoned in a field and decided they would like the plane to be their classroom! The school bought the plane, had it remodelled and fitted with desks. The school reports that attendance has improved dramatically after the aeroplane became a part of the school.

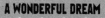

YOUNG POETS' CORNER

A WONDERFUL DREAM

Early one morning, while out to play
I kicked the ball far away
After the ball I ran and ran
And at last when I caught it
I looked up and stared
I saw what I had never seen before
A beautiful countryside - no factories, no cars
No smoke, no sorrow, no hatred, no wars
Only the most merry and loving people in all the lands
I wondered what it would feel like to live in a world like this....
Tring..Tring..Confound that blasted alarm, I said Poof!
That was the end of the most
wonderful dream

Poem sent by
Chloe Fernandes, Pune

PLANT A TREE

Plant a tree, plant a tree
Keep the environment pollution free
In the hot summer blaze, trees offer us
shade
So if you cut one of them
Remember to plant more than ten
Since we depend on trees for life
We should try to keep them alive
Because if all the trees die
Then to heaven we also fly
For animals, trees are shelter
For us, they are food
So treat them like family
And don't be rude
Plant a tree, plant a tree
Make the environment pollution free
Life is not possible without trees
So try to grow them in ones, twos and threes

Poem sent by
Aditi Kulkarni, Mumbai

THANK YOU, BOOKS

I'm going to have a test the next day,
So Mother tells me not to play
She says, 'Baby, sit and read your books
While I clean the floor and cook the food'
The next day when I reach school
The first period is spent in the pool
Then comes the time of the test
And my friends wish me all the best
Later, while eating honey and jam tarts
The teacher comes and gives us our marks
She tells me that I've done extremely well
Just then goes the final bell
'Thank you, books!' I say to myself
'I couldn't have done it without your help!'

Poem sent by
Shilpita Mathews,

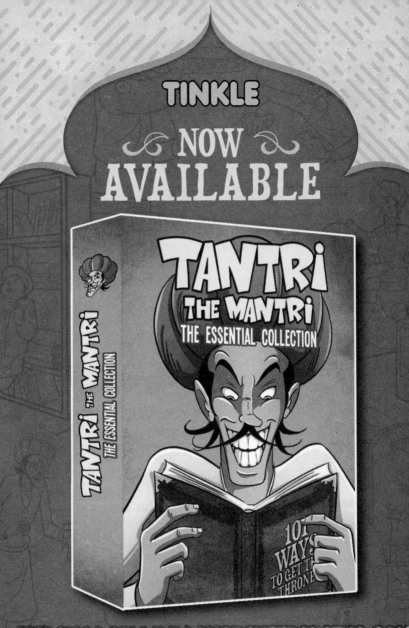

www.tinkleonline.com

70

The Elephant and the Mouse

Story: Alagammai Lakshamanan
Script: Anomita Guha
Illustrations: Prachi Killekar

77

The Human Species

Script: L. Prabhu   Illustrations and Colouring: Jitendra Patil

Sparrows, crows and ostriches are all birds but they belong to different species.

Similarly there are different species of fish and insects. Among the higher animals, though there are only two or three species of elephant, there are nearly two hundred species of monkey and five species of ape.

Are there different species of humans? No, all humans today, whether they are Aborigines of Australia, Eskimos of Alaska or blue-eyed, blond natives of Scandinavia, belong to the same species, *Homo sapiens*.

Chinese

Asian

Caucasian

African

However, there may have been different species of humans in the past. In Europe, *Homo sapiens* and another human species, *Homo neanderthalensis* lived side by side until about 30,000 years ago. Though *Homo neanderthalensis* is believed to have had a brain as large as a present day man's, or even slightly larger, the species for some reason did not survive.

Homo neanderthalensis buried their dead.

In September 2003, Australian and Indonesian scientists excavating on the Indonesian island of Flores stumbled upon fossils of a hitherto unknown human species. This species, since named *Homo floresiensis* (after the island) comprised individuals whose adult height did not exceed that of a modern 4 or 5-year-old child. Their brain size was comparable to that of a chimpanzee.

Early member of our species, Homo sapiens.

They had *Homo sapiens* as neighbours (on other islands), and the two species of humans lived in close proximity to each other as late as 12,000 years ago. Scientists say there may have been populations of small humans in other parts of the world too. This may have given rise to legends of gnomes, elves, leprechauns and other small people who feature in fairytales and folklore.

A Homo floresiensis adult might have looked like this.

TINKLE FUN TIME

(I) Little Shambu has just asked Little Shanti a riddle. To help Little Shanti solve the riddle, cross out all the words meaning 'to laugh' in the jumble below.

AGIGGLELOTSMIRK
GUFFAWOFCHUCKLE
GRINBLOODSMILE
SNIGGERTESTS

WHAT DOES A PHYSICIAN ORDER WHEN HE SUSPECTS THAT YOU HAVE CAUGHT AN INFECTION?

???

(II) Wooly Woo has found a mysterious sequence of five symbols. Can you use logic to help our favourite dragon identify what symbol comes next? Hint: Think of mirror images.

a. b. c.
d. e. f. ?

LEARN HOW A HURRICANE WORKS!

Hurricanes are huge storms that form over tropical oceans. The clouds in a hurricane can be seen as circular bands that spiral around the eye (the calm centre) of the hurricane. You may not have seen a real hurricane, but this experiment lets you see how one works!

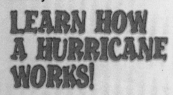

You will need:

A large round bowl of water, an eye dropper, food colouring or watercolours and a spoon.

How to go about it:

1. Stir the water vigorously, moving your spoon in a circular motion.

2. When the water is moving fast, stop stirring.

3. Immediately squeeze several drops of food colouring (or watercolours) into the centre of the bowl.

4. The colour will move out from the centre, forming circular bands.

Clouds in a hurricane swirl around the hurricane's eye in the very same way!

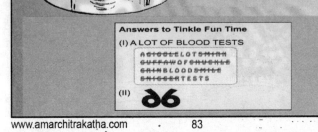

Answers to Tinkle Fun Time

(I) A LOT OF BLOOD TESTS

A~~SIGGLE~~LOT~~SMIRK~~
~~GUFFAW~~OF~~CHUCKLE~~
~~GRIN~~BLOOD~~SMILE~~
~~SNIGGER~~TESTS

(II) 86

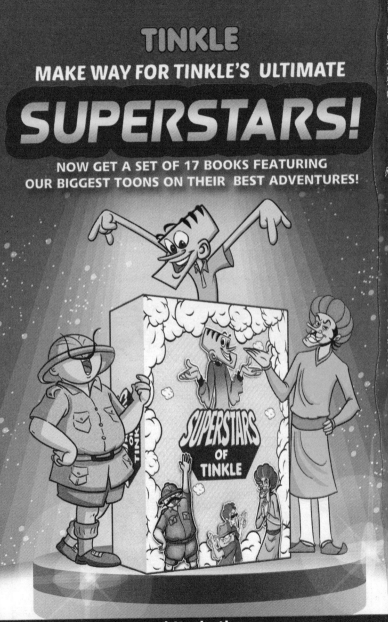